TAKING CARE OF
BUSINESS

A collection of serious and satirical blogs for the 21st Century Entrepreneur.

John Flett

(Publication & copyright details)

© Copyright 2017 John Flett

All rights reserved

No part of this book may be reproduced or transmitted in any form or by means, electronic or mechanical, including photocopying, recording or by any information storage and retrieval system, without permission in writing from the copyright owner.

Printing History

First published January 2017, Lulu Publishing.

"John has an uncanny knack of identifying the real issues and challenges that we face in business every day; and then he shows us what to do about it. With style, humour and depth of knowledge that clearly show his breadth of experience, his writing is engaging, informative and inspiring. This book is for anyone who owns, runs or works in a Business - really is something for everyone."

David Holland, International Business Coach, Author of over 40 business books, Mentor to the Stars.

"John is a vault of knowledge and can recall best practice or solution almost on the fly. John has a your-friend-in-the-boardroom approach but if needed he takes no prisoners. His only goal appears to be, to get me to my goal, by whatever means necessary. My only regret, I didn't meet John earlier! This book encapsulates John's knowledge and if you are not a great reader, it has been made easy with short, punchy chapters filled with great advice."

Anthony Fensom, Director at Consulting IT (Client).

"In the years that John has been involved with what was originally Waltons Wood Products John has helped transform the business to a modern forward thinking profitable 21st Century Business. This book captures the essence of what John is all about. A great little book which has been written in a way that is easy to read, and portrays John's sense of humour as well!"

David Steven, General Manager at Express Pallets Pty Ltd.

This book is dedicated to my four gorgeous children
Diane, Ronnie, Sonja and Terry.

Contents

Acknowledgements	viii
Introduction	x
Why Micromanaging Causes Fear in the Workplace	1
Do You Dread Coming to Work?	4
The One Big Problem in the Workplace	9
Fear in the Workplace	12
Dumb Micromanaging and Stupid Emails	16
Motivating Employees	19
Don't Look Back	22
Success?	25
What is Your Story?	28
Gossip	31
How Do I Stop Being Micromanaged?	33
The Right Way	36
Training That is Never Implemented	39
Compassion	42
The Power of Intention	44
A Bully in a Sneaky Disguise?	47
Great Employee vs One That Should Be Employed Elsewhere	51
Books for the 21st Century	55
Looking for Work/Life Solution	59
Negotiation	62

Acknowledgements

My life experiences have taught me such a lot. However, without the help of my many friends along the way, the education and the up-to-date knowledge gained through reading (my goal being to read one book a week), I would not be where I am today.

Today I am so grateful to all my Business Coaching clients, many of whom have achieved success both personally and professionally beyond their wildest dreams through working with me, some who have taught me lessons that were unexpected and others who still ring me long after the coaching has ended, just to keep me up-to date on their new achievements.

I am constantly inspired and motivated by my own Business Coach. Dave you are a living legend! You both walk the walk and talk the talk, being the perfect role model. I thank my beautiful partner, Heather who supports my pursuits and works alongside me to help make things happen. The sound of her steps on the back stairs still makes my heart flutter when she arrives home! My children and grandchildren who are all amazing, beautiful and intelligent, thank you for being just you.

A massive thank you also to the following:

Paul van Barneveld of Brave Creative, who changed my perception of branding – done properly and to a depth that I had never been aware of before. The results speak for themselves with the new brand ScopeBC, the brilliant book cover design, and much much more.

Julie and Felicity of Audacious Digital for the production, implementation and design of the new website, the promotion of this book as well as the social media.

Claire of Paramount Video for the video production and photos.

Elaine, Dean, the list goes on and on. Thank you all. I am incredibly grateful for all the support you have given me and continue to.

To my friends – I won't name you but you know who you are – thank you.

Introduction

The road that led me to becoming a business coach 10 years ago, was borne out of both my own learning and extensive business experience. It never fails to bring me joy to see my clients step into increased business success through my coaching. I remain constantly motivated to show them how to use their innate talents to build even stronger, thriving businesses, reaching far beyond their initial expectations.

I was born in the town of Crieff in Scotland and with a then population of 6,000 I was fortunate to have a fantastic schooling at Morrisons Academy and was privileged to go to school with a wide variety of children from overseas as well as local. This set the stage at an early age for viewing business on the international arena.

Selling was in my blood, and at 14 I was thrust into selling door to door the excess fruit which my sisters couldn't sell to the local shop. Next came business number two, selling tablecloths. This involved buying rolls of plastic tablecloth, cutting them up into appropriate lengths and after three tablecloths the rest was pure profit! Sadly, one of my sisters got married and moved overseas to live, we had to sell the business in a hurry, and I now know that it wasn't exit ready. Although we still made a nice little profit, I knew we could have done better.

In despair at my passion for business, my father sent me off to college to learn to be an Accountant so that at least I would know what I was doing as I was still determined to be a businessman.

As it turned out I was never cut out for Accountancy, but the knowledge learnt helped greatly with my businesses.

Soon after, I started a business – a proper business installing and servicing Air Compressors. At first it was a sideline to my job, but it soon grew to fulltime and spread throughout Scotland. After 11 years in business, I decided to broaden my horizons, so I sold up completely and moved myself and my family to Australia. In 1990, loaded up with 26 suitcases, we emigrated to Brisbane which has been home ever since.

However, once again, the business was not exit ready, and although very profitable, when it came to selling, it was at a reduced price! I spotted the pattern from earlier experience and it has fuelled my passion to not only get it right for myself but to help other business owners to get their businesses in order and exit ready for a great return at sale time.

Working in Australia soon brought international travel opportunities with new challenges and learnings. I now coach my business clients locally and internationally based out of Brisbane, host events and do speaking engagements.

2017 heralds a new beginning for my company, with rebranding to more accurately reflect my values and philosophy.

ScopeBC offers business coaching and consultancy services designed to assist business owners to grow their businesses and to overcome barriers to success. This book will give you an overview of my commitment to helping people to gain greater rewards in their businesses with less effort. I look forward to talking with you, and if the fit is right, working with you to achieve this.

John Flett

john@scopebc.com.au

— CHAPTER 1 —
Why Micromanaging Causes Fear in the Workplace

Micromanaging diminishes your self-worth. When someone is micromanaging you, it spells to you that:

a) They don't trust you

b) They are probably putting you down, and attempting to lower your self-esteem, and boost theirs instead.

c) As by their actions of micromanaging and showing their lack of trust, it generates fear in you because you're thinking goes to imagining that you are going to get the sack, be transferred or given less hours; you freeze and go into protection mode.

Because of the actions of your boss and being frozen with fear, your cognitive abilities go out the window, you make silly errors you wouldn't normally do, and the boss calmly and smugly congratulates himself – as this is his proof that you needed micromanaging. It also increases his busyness and looking important to his seniors.

Avoid micromanaging at all costs.

There is something basically wrong in the organisation if there are insufficient systems to protect the company without the need of micromanaging. Micromanaging is a brilliant way to destroy a great culture in an incredibly short space of time.

Micromanaging *destroys* trust! Trust can take years to build and 30 seconds to destroy. It also destroys discretionary effort and turns the team into little zombies who are afraid of everything.

So *where* do these micromanagers come from? Usually the temptation is to employ people like yourself. If one of the directors who is in charge of hiring is a micromanager watch out!

Of course, we get influenced by the media and the dear old governments around the world. The media and governments love to spread fear, and want us all to live in little micromanaged bubbles.

What have the *raspberries* got to do with it I hear you say? Well are there six there or seven? You are wrong is what the micromanager says. Check again. Check again. Check again. Belittling you and being told you are wrong is awful.

Is there ever a time for micromanaging? Sure. When someone is learning, they need to be micromanaged until they have learnt the process, system or procedure. But how you do that must be on a curve that leads them to self-empowerment.

You also need to micromanage when there is the suspicion of gross misconduct such as suspected fraud or other serious issues going on.

So why do some bosses persistently micromanage? Often it is because they are filled with fear themselves. Full of what ifs. They are also worried and fearful about what others think. What other people think of course is none of their business!

Lao Tzu, Chinese philosopher wrote, 'Care about what other people think and you will always be their prisoner.'

Micromanagers are not happy. Impossible to be happy, as they are racked by fear. They are spreading fear. The best place for them is away from people and dealing with figures which must be deadly accurate. Then when they have micromanaged their way through these figures, tell them that they are a 100% correct, and if you are lucky you may get a smile and they will definitely tell you that they knew that.

The Micromanager will also complain that none of his team will take responsibility for their work and actions, and has the giant scotoma that he or she is the one to blame!

They are also 'parenting' their team, which automatically draws out the reaction of childish behaviour with their team, and the consequence is that both parties go home exhausted and frustrated at the day's end.

– CHAPTER 2 –

Do You Dread Coming to Work?

Even the cat or dog gets a dirty look as you walk out the door to go to work.

Do you find as you start getting nearer and nearer to your workplace, the body starts making protests? The joints start to stiffen and you don the 'work look'. A bit hunched up in protection mode. That is *not normal*!

The sad fact is that there are far too many workplaces where a whole long list of abnormal activities is passed off as being normal, or at least okay 'in the corporate world'. One hears comments made such as, 'Man up mate, you are in the corporate world now,' as though the problem lies with you, and not the perpetrator(s).

This list is not comprehensive and I would be interested to find out what you have experienced or have seen around your workplace.

Here is a list of what I have witnessed/experienced:

1. Workplace bullying
2. Fear
3. Micromanaging
4. Passive aggressive behaviour
5. Manipulative negotiation
6. Laughing loudly by certain employees at the boss's pathetic jokes to curry his/her favour

7. Nepotism
8. Entrapment
9. Gossip
10. Favouritism. Employing or promoting staff based on looks, gender, race or age. For example 'pretty girl' being promoted over a person who was much better qualified and suited for the promotion.
11. Toxic culture
12. Coercive behaviour quietly approved by management.
13. Someone was successful in 1999, so therefore they are still wonderful and amazing today (in case you missed it that was a sarcastic comment!) Which leads onto,
14. Sarcasm

What is going to *change* this type of behaviour and when will it happen?

Part of the work I do involves dramatic and different ways of changing the environment of the workplace. When I walk into a business premise I unfortunately come across and *feel* the toxicity! You can almost *smell* it!

Picture the poor workers subjected to this daily!

Your heart goes out to them.

Are you a true Leader or just a Boss? A true Leader thinks. Not just sometimes, but *all* the time. What impact are you having on your fellow worker? What impact are they having on you? An acceptance of mediocrity (at best), is not something we should settle for. It also amazes me that owners, CEOs are blissfully unaware sometimes as to what is going on with their team!

One sure sign of a bad work environment is the revolving door – a continuous staff turnover, seven leaving, seven working, and seven joining. This is something I have seen, experienced and continue to observe with some incredulity that the CEO still regards that as normal!

CEOs listen up, are there *stories* coming out of your HR department, and are they backed up with what their feet are telling you?

The feet don't lie.

The most honest of tell-tale signs is what the feet are doing.

For more detail, read Joe Navarro (Ex CIA Interrogator)'s book 'WHAT EVERY BODY IS SAYING'.

Check out what your own feet are doing next time that you are in an uncomfortable situation. Are they squirming one shoe on top of the ankle of the other? If your employee's feet are pointing *towards the exit door*, it may well mean that they are heading towards another job!

From years of experience, it is my firm belief that in most workplaces at least one of the above is going on. It must stop! Perhaps the boss doesn't realise that because of her/his attitude, demeanour and interaction with the team, the team members are operating at between 5 and 40% discretionary effort. In other words, they are operating at a level just above avoiding being sacked. Some of these workers even resort to subversive behaviours as a means of 'getting even', with practices such as sabotage and theft not uncommon.

Another problem is treating your employees as cogs in a wheel, and not verifying that they are the right fit for the job. That necessarily involves personality profiling – a subject that I am particularly passionate about, and do with all my clients without exception. As Jim Collins puts so eloquently in his book GOOD TO GREAT, and I paraphrase in my own words– get the wrong people off the bus, the right people in the right seats on the bus, before you even decide *where you are going*!

Why put an outgoing 'people person' in a back office with no social interaction, doing detailed paperwork all day? Then you wonder why he/she is demoralised!

The other problem is misinformation. I refer especially to two documents. Firstly, *the annual performance review*.

What effect does the annual performance review have on the already stressed out employee, as well as her equally stressed out supervisor/boss/team leader? 'Oh, but we have always done it; I had to do it all these years ago,' the boss may say in defence of the practice.

Yes, and what did it do to improve *anything?* We seem to forget that we are in the times of constant never-ending massive change, and the old 'dinosaur' performance review should have been buried along with its analytically obsessed creator 50 years ago!

The next one is the *exit interview*. Do you honestly think that you are going to get the truth from an employee who is leaving? Really? Mostly they will tell you what you want to hear. 'Just let me get out the door Sunshine, and I'll tell you what you want to hear… Yes, I left for more money, not because of you, you old witch,' is what may be going through their heads.

In contrast have the following three questions been asked:

1. What *outcome* will we get from this performance review?
2. What *outcome* will we get from this exit interview?
3. What am I going to *change* as a *result* of the completion of the above two documents?

It would be nice to think that with these changes in place, your journey to work would be a pleasant one!

– CHAPTER 3 –

The One Big Problem in the Workplace

There is only one big problem in the workplace.

To explain what it is, I am first going to tell you a story.

This morning we went for a lovely breakfast at a different venue to the one we usually go to. The food was great, the coffee was excellent and we started chatting to the owner. During the conversation, he asked what I did, and he took a step back when I told him what it is. I could read his thoughts from the look on his face – 'Uh! A Business Coach? I don't want one of those! I know everything and besides that costs money!' It was a conversation killer. However, as I observed his place, his demeanour and his attitude, I knew that that he didn't qualify to work with me.

I carried on with the conversation, and offered to give him a couple of bits of free advice, which he grudgingly agreed to listen to.

You see, cafes and coffee shops are easy to coach, unless there is one big problem. It is the same problem in my coaching business and it is the same problem in your life whether you are a CEO, employee or self-employed.

Now take a hard look at yourself, and I will let you into the secret. The secret is *you*, (or in my case – *me*), because sad to say, I think I know it all! Oh bother!

Is that *it* I hear you say?

Well, I'll go back to my coffee shop man again. I told him about another coffee shop owner I helped a few years ago, and she told me she couldn't afford me. I told her she couldn't afford not to have me, and I offered her a wager, which she took.

The wager was that if I could prove to her that I wouldn't cost her a cent, would I get the gig? She agreed, so when I asked her how many cups of coffee she sold in a certain period she replied proudly 1200 cups, which at that time she sold for $3.60 a cup. The cost price of the coffee including rent, wages, breakages, cost of the coffee, sugar and milk worked out at 41 cents.

'Gather round your team please and from now on this is what they are going to do,' I said. As they take away the dirty cups, smile, and while nodding cheerily say, 'Same again Ma'am, same again Sir?' Nod, nod. The customers will look at each other and go 'oh, what the heck okay'. When she later put it into practice, she sold another 800 cups of coffee. The result? Let's round up the 41 cents for easy Math and call it 60 cents. $3.00 x 800 cups. $2400 extra pure profit!

'Am I costing you no money and are you making a heap more Ma'am, yes or yes?' She had to agree. I got the gig!!!

First coffees finished, and now into the second one, I gave my coffee shop owner another free coaching tip. 'You have empty walls so why don't you invite a local struggling artist to display their work and go 50/50 on whatever sells? Pure extra profit.'

'Oh, no we can't do that, I tried that once before and the artist had her hand in the till', he replied.

Why do you think this gentleman does not qualify to work with me as his Business Coach?

It is the same reason some busy CEOs are far too busy to see me as they are very, very, busy in busy, busy, busyness, and they know everything anyway.

It may be the same reason that your boss micromanages you, because he knows it all, and well, (polite cough...) not-so-deep down he doesn't trust you because he knows it all.

Now if you have read this far in this chapter, give yourself a pat on the back because you are getting the drift.

If I have an 'I know it all' attitude I am impossible to help or coach!

That is the one problem in the workplace today!

– CHAPTER 4 –
Fear in the Workplace

Few business owners spend the time to think about what effect fear is having in the workplace. I am on a mission to change this for every good reason.

If fear is taking place at your work it is affecting a lot of things, not least of which is health.

It also affects greatly harmonious working, and the ability for the team to express ideas and thoughts which they may have that would improve the common good.

Let's look at fear and see what it is and what it does. When we get hit with fear it causes certain reactions in the brain and body. First, and this is where I disagree with the fight/flight popularised theory, we freeze. Think of a bank hold up with people captured in it. Their first reaction is to freeze. They don't go into fight mechanism first. Ok, after the initial freeze some may run like crazy!

What happens when this fear is activated is we get a release of adrenalin into our blood-stream? The amygdala or reptile primitive brain takes over, blood drains from the cognitive part of our brains (in other words we can't think straight), and the oxygen is pumped to our muscle groups in readiness for flight (probably) second, and fight, a distant third.

At work, if we keep the fear going all day, cortisol, the stress hormone takes over, and aided and abetted by more adrenalin pumps, and caffeine hits, we get through the day.

Cortisol was the stress hormone needed by our ancestors to keep going in the hunt for wild animals to kill and bring back to their tribe. Today, it takes away the muscle around our bellies and replaces it with a large layer of protective fat as we have no bones there to protect us from the fear our boss is throwing at us. Of course, that gives us more stress as I know of no one who wants a fatter belly!

On a more positive note, and thanks to the excellent work of Professor Mihaly Csikszentmihalyi, there is a better way. Read his books Creativity and Flow. A word of warning first – you will need your thesaurus open as he uses words not usually heard outside University circles!

Not written as a 'pop' personal development book, he has explained flow. Flow is that sweet spot we have all had at some stage in our lives where time becomes irrelevant and everything just flows beautifully.

You cannot reach flow in a workplace riddled with fear, bullying, gossip, coercive manipulations, innuendos and mischievous behaviours.

Put simply, is your workplace a place where fear is going on? If it is, it is costing millions and possibly billions of dollars. It is also making you sick.

Detecting the presence of fear can be as simple as noting a company's inability to retain staff. Unhappiness causes people to leave, and often – because of fear – they don't really let rip and tell the owners what is going on, as they depart the building.

Statistics show that in America, an estimated 88% of the workforce (approximately 130 million people) go home every day feeling that they work for an organisation that doesn't listen or care about them. That is seven out of eight people! *(Source www.maritz.com/media/files Executive Summary Research pdf from the book Everybody Matters by Bob Chapman and Raj Sisodia published 2015).* If similar research was done here in Australia, I am sure the results would not be much different. Every member of my family has been subjected to fear through bullying in the workplace at some stage in our careers.

Fear causes mistakes to happen in the workplace. We know that the reptilian brain has taken over and, without cognitive functions working properly, clear decision-making is impossible. Consequentially, these mistakes compromise bottom-line profit.

The interesting thing is, the bottom line profit which CEOs and shareholders are besotted with, increases dramatically when you get rid of fear in the workplace!

The problem is that many CEOs are in denial of the damaging effects of fear. When they refuse to change their way of thinking, their employees walk, again and again and again.

There is a popularised theory that Gen Ys and Gen Is leave anyway after 18 months on average, and that there is nothing you can do about it. I say that is rubbish. Look hard within, for the real reason. If you want them to stay, and more importantly be constructive, happy, motivated and free of fear, then YOU must change. Get rid of fear in your workplace!

Think about what causes fear. If you are suspicious of men in grey suits who have suddenly started to turn up in your office, gossip starts – 'are we being taken over? Are they doing due diligence? What if…? How will I be able to get another job? My boss laughed at me the other day and the innuendo was I would never get another job because I am over fifty!' These are the sort of statements and questions you have heard I am sure.

Fear fuels gossip, panic and unrest. Gossip is a subject covered later in the book, as it is another one right up there in destroying not only companies but people's lives.

— CHAPTER 5 —
Dumb Micromanaging and Stupid Emails

Big brother is watching you!

I have written quite a bit about micromanaging, but it is a little bit different when you experience it. It was a harsh wakeup call when it happened to me recently.

My partner and I volunteered to help at a weekend conference and experienced micromanaging alive and kicking, and every bit as bad as when I first experienced it many years ago.

It was horrible. Demeaning. Rude. Tempting us into being childish in response.

Spend enough time under micromanaging, and discretionary effort would go pretty much to zero.

It also leads to doubling up, and you find that you are doing the same job as someone else who has been asked by the micromanager to do it as well, for what reason?

It doesn't make sense. What puzzles me is that there are managers out there still trying to justify themselves for micromanaging, and blaming 'the system' for persisting in this vile habit.

Quite amazing!

So why do managers persist with this awful habit?

A big slab of ego may also be part of the problem. While discussing this in casual conversation this morning, with a trusted professional, he commented that one of the reasons he felt they did it, was to prove how 'busy' they were; they wrote more emails than anyone else in the organisation; sent out 5 emails when one carefully constructed one would have done the job better. A fair and unfortunately accurate point.

Which draws me to the next point – stupid emails.

Stupid emails are the ones that have RE as the subject line followed by other ones with FYI. You then open them and discover your name and every man and his dog's email addresses have been blabbed to the world, as they have been cc'd into it.

Even more annoying are the ones that leave you scratching your head as they are so convoluted you wonder what the point is, and what the sender wants you to do.

People like to read mysteries, not live them.

That applies to meetings too. My micromanaging 'friend' also told me to attend a meeting. 'What is the meeting about?' I inquired politely. 'Don't worry. It won't take long,' he said. That is the politician's reply. Reply to a different question. Perhaps you can guess that by this time I was getting annoyed! Persisting, I tried another line. 'What outcome do you want from this meeting?' to which I received, 'What is wrong with you? It won't take long!'

Going on the basis that you don't try to educate idiots, as they will only drag you down to their level and beat you with experience, I then made the decision to go elsewhere.

If you are arranging a meeting, tell people what it is about, what the intended outcome of the meeting is, have an agenda and keep to it! Remember, transparent, focussed outcomes are best and less is more. That way the whole team will be prepared and on the same page before they even get to the meeting.

As you can see, the agenda is a powerful tool and it is worth the while constructing it in advance of your meeting. The very fact of circulating the agenda with the outcome you want, sometimes negates the need of the meeting completely!

On a side note, it bewilders me that a manager can call a one hour meeting for 12 people, just to check in with everyone, possibly costing the company $1000 plus in wages, without reference to senior authority, and yet the same person must get authority to spend $100! Now that's dumb micromanaging all round!!

– CHAPTER 6 –
Motivating Employees

In any interaction with an employee, think of it from their perspective first. I believe Jim Rohn was credited with saying that in a sales conversation look to answer your client's needs first. Similarly, the same applies to your employees.

The *wrong* question to ask yourself is:

What do I have to say to make my employees work harder and more intelligently?

The *right* question to ask yourself is:

What focus, guidance, better understanding and clarity do I need to give *them* for them to use their abilities more intelligently?

Whenever I hear about business owners talking about *managing* their people, I cringe. You can't *manage* people – especially Gen Ys and Gen Is. Forget it! They walk.

You can only *lead* your team. Talking *at* them instead of talking *with* them is a common mistake. However, if you are treating your team like little cogs in a machine, get ready for high staff turnover.

Manage your tasks, but *not* your team.

If in your organisation people are constantly leaving, and you are in a responsible management position for hiring and firing, stop and think. Think a lot harder than you have before, as you may find that if you take responsibility for the situation, you may just start to find the answer.

The funny thing is, that in my life whenever there has been a problem, one constant has always remained – I was there every time!! Quite annoying eh! Talk *with*, not *at* your team members.

We all know that the ultimate basis for doing any kind of business is *trust*. So, there is a process for that to come about, and it amuses me to see people who try to short circuit this process.

Certain steps are necessary to provide trust whether it is with employees or with clients.

It starts with laser focus. That focus then provides clarity. Clarity provides the power to gain understanding. Understanding gives certainty. Certainty when underpinned with genuine integrity gives trust.

Let's reflect on ourselves, and in your case, yourself and for me, myself. Am I basically honest?

Am I working with 100% integrity?

Integrity is doing the right thing when there is nobody else there watching.

If you have no integrity you have nothing. As a metaphor consider the game of tennis. 98% over the net is a fail. 100% over the net is essential.

The same applies to running your business. 100% honesty and 100% integrity is essential and is the only sure way to build an enduring relationship with your employees, and a long lasting one with your clients and suppliers.

We know that all things being equal people *buy* from people they know like and trust; all things *not* being equal, people still buy from people they know, like and trust.

Employees are no different. They need to know, like and trust you, if you are going to get their buy-in to what you want them to do, when you are *not* there, as well as when you are there supervising them. It also means, that if they know, like and trust you, and a job offer comes along and the much higher wage they are offered you can't match, they may well stay even though it is an unequal playing field.

Just to recap. Inspiring and motivating employees is vital for the success of any business. Talking *with* them and not *at* them is a good start, but you must prove yourself completely honest and show integrity first in order to build genuine trust.

– CHAPTER 7 –
Don't Look Back

Don't look back. Cute little lamb though...

You are not going that way, and if you keep looking back you are going to trip up and fail or fall.

What ifs, should haves could haves, going tos, in the past we dids..., buts, and you have to understands, are pet hates of mine.

Look ahead. Look as far as you can, and the how tos will come to you. So many people get bogged down, turn back and will not accept that *change* is the new normal.

Massive change is the new normal, in fact.

No such thing as failure – just market feedback and learnings that you would not have got any other way.

The point is that armed with such useful feedback we can look ahead with renewed confidence that at least we don't have to try that again.

'But you must understand, John, I wanted to go to University and get a degree and I can't afford to.' What ifs don't cut it.

Look for alternatives. Can you download the free Kindle app and learn from that? Yes, of course. Can you afford a few dollars to buy a few decent books? Of course, you can, and some of them are free too. If that is too hard, you can go to your local library and borrow books for free. How easy is that to continue your education?

'But I don't have time to read books' may be a nice little excuse. Do you travel to and from work? Yes, and could you listen to audio books on the way there and back instead of listening to rubbish on the car radio?

Do you watch the news? If you said yes, I can save you the trouble and tell you the news for the next twenty years! The government is terrible, the violence is getting worse, then there is the sport and your team either won, lost or drew, and the ref was rubbish. Then the weather is either terrible for being too hot, too cold, wet or dry. There you are – another hour you can spend reading!

University on the other hand, may not be your answer. I see people enrolling for MBAs – one graduate bragging to me that his executive MBA had cost him over $100,000!

Hmm, now I don't want to upset people and would just like to ask the question, what part of your University degree course are you using now? Just asking.

You need to ensure that you receive VALUE! Give VALUE and receive VALUE! Increase your own value through learning. Not through using the latest buzz words, and bumping your gums about them.

One of the biggest problems is when we think we know it all.

Especially, if we have had a measure of success.

That is a sinister trap that so many people fall into, and is the fast route to stagnation in life and business, and in some cases major disaster. A trap with letters after your name can sucker you in as well.

It is one of the reasons I have a Business Coach. 'But John, you are a great Business Coach yourself. Why on earth do you have one?' some people ask me.

It is because I want to keep adding value to myself, and in turn be able to share with my clients, plus keep me grounded and in touch with cutting edge new changes in this ever-changing world we live in. I also get a different perspective and accountability. Plus…honest feedback – the breakfast of champions- Ken Blanchard (The One Minute Manager). My Coach also is my sounding board and someone I know is 110% committed to my success. Very nice to have someone like that on your team. Worth it unquestionably.

– CHAPTER 8 –

Success?

Success – How do you measure it?

What is success?

Is success a trap?

The tendency is that when peers, parents, teachers and friends tell us that money is not a measure of someone's success, secretly we disagree. When you see how people grovel and slobber over the likes of Richard Branson or Tony Robbins you know that we not-so-secretly actually do believe that money is what it is all about.

Sad but true.

What are you chasing?

If it is purely money and you are hell bent on that, there is a fair chance that you may get it.

You may also get and lose a few other things you didn't bargain for along the way too.

Whenever I start with a new client, I always ask them what they want. It never fails to amaze me that many, many times they proceed to tell me all the things they don't want!

Oh, we are weird eh!

The fact is that what we focus on we get more of.

Perhaps if we looked at our values and what we cherish deeply and highly, then that would be a smarter way of looking at success. Look at Mother Theresa, was she successful? Sure, she was. But was she financially loaded in cash? Not that I am aware of. Isn't that interesting!

Because always bear in mind that your own resolve to gain success is more important than any one thing.

The last question I raised was 'Is success a trap?'

In recent observations, I have noticed this problem time and time again. When we get to a measure of success – nice house, car, possessions, money in the bank, kids at good schools and doing well, healthy and business rolling along, we are in a crucial area of thinking that because we are 'successful' we no longer need to heed advice. We may even feel qualified to dish out our own advice instead!

The awareness of this success trap is what fuels me to keep learning, keep listening, engaging, reading and last, but by no means least, *observing*.

Keep up to date. Do you know about Blockchain? If you don't know, google it and learn.

Observing strengthens you. Judging weakens you. While someone else's measure of success is up to them, let's not judge them. They are just on a different path. However, I believe that it is helpful to observe them.

Ponder. Think. So many people don't think, and their success is tainted. We even have people calling themselves 'Thought Leaders' now. What the heck is that about?

Do you need someone else to do your thinking for you? Dear oh dear, what next? One problem in the modern world is that we have got into the way of thinking that if we can't come up with the answer instantly, then we need someone else to do our thinking for us. Give it time. Letting a difficult problem roll around in your own head often produces amazing answers and consequently results.

However, if you are still not getting the results and successes you desire, you will need a good Coach, Mentor or someone else who can give you a different perspective. Think of an ant's perspective compared to yours looking at the same object – vastly different, and it is no different in your life and business.

If you want to be more successful in your life, however you define it, do get in touch. My passion is helping people just like you to achieve the success in your life whatever your path. Because in the words of a famous brand – You are worth it!

– CHAPTER 9 –
What is Your Story?

What are the shoes doing there?

Whose shoes are they?

How long have they been there?

The heels are very high, so I bet she had sore feet and just took them off and left them there. What a waste of money as they look quite new. Maybe she had an argument with her boyfriend and ran off without them.

These stories plus a few more went through my head when I came across this scenario recently, and it made me think of all the different stories we tell ourselves about everything.

We do it every day. Once having made up our own little story about what is happening around us, we then set about reinforcing that belief. Sometimes of course our stories may be quite wrong, but human nature being what it is, we hate being found out to be wrong! In fact, in my humble opinion, one of the things that upsets people the most is when someone says *'you are wrong!'* Oh, we all hate that. We really can't handle that.

There is often a *story* made up in the mind of that person, reinforced with negative core beliefs, and to get that person to change their story is a mighty task.

If we want to grow and learn, we need to think *differently*. Everything starts there. One of the expressions I don't like is when someone says, 'John, you have to understand that in our business, that can't work.' It is very easy to focus on all the things that won't work, and much harder work to focus on coming up with something that may work.

Unlike animals, the other favourite thing us humans do is love jumping to the worst conclusion. 'Oh, these shoes must have been left by someone who had jumped off the bridge!'

Really? How do you know that was the case? What ifs, should haves, might haves, might still happens, scared, fear-filled thoughts don't help anyone. Animals don't do that. In fact, quite the opposite. Once it's over red rover, it's over.

What has this got to do with my business I hear you ask? Perhaps if we changed our *perspective* from a *negative* one to a *positive* one, just for a start, then we may start to see different results. I help my clients with that.

Studies were done on popular music. They found that when the music genre was upbeat, the economies of the world went better. So perhaps when listening to music, it's better to listen to D.Ream *THINGS CAN ONLY GET BETTER* than Nirvana's *TEEN SPIRIT!*

The fact is that we are telling ourselves stories every day. Would it not be a good idea when telling ourselves these stories, to be sure we tell ourselves *good* ones.

The same applies to questions. What if we only asked ourselves *better* questions? Would we not get *better* answers and *better* results?

Of course, we would.

As a footnote, these shoes were sitting perched on the parapet of a bridge in Prague, Czech Republic, and may have been placed there as a reminder of what happened to the Jews during World War 2.

However, that is just a *story*!

Feel free to write me if you have a better *story* about them.

– CHAPTER 10 –
Gossip

A little talked about problem that bugs many a business is gossip. Gossip is none of your business!

A 60+ year old lady I knew commented to me one fine day about her daughter, who was in her early 40's. Mature, stable and doing the best she could with her young family after having been dumped by her husband, she had started dating a new man.

Mother was not amused! As she ranted on gossiping about her daughter, I felt compelled to say, 'Hey, stop a minute. This is gossip and it is none of your business.' 'Oh!' she replied, 'I was speaking to someone else about this and they said the same thing. My tarot card reader, and she told me as well!'

'*It is none of your business*!'

As I observed her slowly beginning to realise that who her daughter dated was none of her business, it occurred to me that the same thing goes on in business in terms of gossip.

Gossip is one of the things that has the potential to destroy a business as well as people's lives. We hear gossip, and then the automatic reaction is to jump to a conclusion and judge.

Gossip fuels judgement.

One of my clients was having huge problems with his team who were gossiping all day and every day. The work was not getting done, they were demotivated, and there was an alarming lack of discretionary effort. So, we came up with a novel solution, and brought in Julius.

Julius was a cardboard box with his name proudly on the outside. Julius looked after the gossip. Brilliant at it! He stayed at the entrance of the workplace, and had a good lid. When one of the team started gossiping, one of the other team members would politely ask that person to write down what she was saying, put it in an envelope for safe-keeping with Julius until 5pm, when she could retrieve it and take her gossip home with her.

Julius was excellent at his job and remained there doing sterling work in keeping the office free of gossip.

Gossip was Julius' business.

You will be pleased to know that Julius is not trademarked and if gossip is a problem around your workplace, you can use your own Julius to sort that out because *gossip is none of your business!*

– CHAPTER 11 –
How Do I Stop Being Micromanaged?

When I started on this journey of helping business owners, I never envisaged educating people on how micromanaging produces fear, which holds back so many good people from having happy, healthy and productive lives.

Our ancestors lived a very simple life. No life insurance. No pension. No internet. They lived in the here and now. Firstly shelter, water and food. And, of course, avoiding being eaten or attacked by wild animals. It did not enter their heads about the what ifs and the future.

Nowadays, we are wracked with fear and anxiety about the future, and where micromanagers starts from, is an intrinsic fear. Often, they are projecting their fear onto you, and I have various tools to deal with that effectively. It takes time and patience as well as acceptance that some people will never change. Simply you are wasting your life trying to change them.

To help you stop being micromanaged, let's have a look at some 21st century tools available for dealing and coping with this problem.

Meditation is now no longer an option. It is mandatory as we are getting bombarded with billions of bits of information every minute, and the human condition being what it is, needs a break. Now, before you get worried, you don't have to sit cross-legged and go 'ohm' all day. Meditating can be as easy as feeding the chooks and daydreaming. But do something.

Liquids consumption. Drink less coffee and tea, and drink more water (not the alcoholic type!) You will be calmer, and more able to observe the behaviour of your micromanager rather than let her/him get inside your head and mess with it. When I cut my coffee intake, it directly led to me becoming less anxious.

Transactional Analysis. Dr Eric Berne and his friend Thomas Harris did a lot of work in this area back in the 1970s with this rather grandiose term 'Transactional Analysis'.

Check out Dr Berne's book, *GAMES PEOPLE PLAY*.

Briefly, it describes interactions and how we address others. We address others in the form of parent, adult or child. If we are addressed as a parent, it evokes the typical automatic response of a child. In turn, because I have been addressed by the parent (usually your micromanager boss), and my automatic response is a child one – such as 'oh sorry, I was just trying my best!'. That in turn evokes the response from your boss of another parental rebuke, which in turn causes you to reply with another childish reply, and so on it goes all day, every day.

The net result is your boss goes home exhausted because he/she has been parenting you all day, and you go home exhausted, frustrated and angry because you have been treated like a little kid all day!

Now there is a lot more to understanding this concept, and please don't think you can master it all in one simple paragraph, because sorting out the workplace dynamics is a key part of what I do. This takes awareness, time and monitoring to produce lasting change.

There may well be other issues at work and a couple of other books I recommend for more understanding on this topic are:

TRICKY PEOPLE. HOW TO DEAL WITH HORRIBLE TYPES BEFORE THEY RUIN YOUR LIFE by Andrew Fuller.

THE OBJECT OF MY AFFECTION IS IN MY REFLECTION, COPING WITH NARCISSISTS by Rokelle Lerner.

– CHAPTER 12 –
The Right Way

The right way, or up the garden path?

Employing people for the first time in your expanding business is more than a big step. It is a *massive* step.

If you rely on crossed fingers and hope, that equates to inviting a disaster. It could cost you your business. I know from harsh experience. The first employee I took on, was a friend's daughter and it was her first job. A friend! Doh! Disaster. Did I learn? Nup. The second one was another friend's son. Yes, you got it. Another disaster! Did I learn then? Well, yes – sort of.

I advertised the next time, and thought I didn't need to worry about reference checks. Who needs them, eh? Well, this employee had a history of theft, helped herself to the petty cash and ran up a massive telephone bill which came in at the end of the quarter just after I sacked her.

Did I learn something then? Oh yes, you betcha. 'All employees are thieves!' was the message I received, and don't tell them anything. Mushroom technique – keep 'em in the dark, and feed 'em sh**.

Are *all* employees like that? *All* the time? Hmm, a bit harsh eh, and yet stumbling through many experiences over many years, I finally developed a *system* which works *most* of the time! Why not every time, I hear you ask? Because we are dealing with humans (the odd alien perhaps?) and it is not an exact science.

The system works very well, when you follow it. If you skip bits, it is like baking a cake and missing a couple of key ingredients, it will inevitably turn to mush.

What system are you using? If you are using something *better* than crossed fingers or employing friends, relatives, friends of relatives, old school mates, cute looking people, or similar then give yourself a pat on the back.

Is the system you are using delivering you the results you want? How long are your new victi..oops employees lasting? Are they exiting just after you've trained them? If that is the case, then where is the trouble coming from?

It is necessary to look at the bigger picture. What is your work *culture* like? If your culture sucks, then it needs to be changed. This is the core of the problem. If, as an employer you find yourself making lots of justifying statements, and you are still unsure of who to blame, step back and re-assess your *leadership style*. Then you will *definitely* know where the problem comes from.

Perhaps you are thinking that your recruiting process is not too bad. You have self-talk including a list of excuses the length of your arm why the hires don't work out. Stop fooling yourself! Life can be so much better. A happy, thriving, buzzing workplace is good for everyone's health. Team happiness, prosperity and achievement of goals are paramount and you'll retain your best workers.

It has taken me years to come up with a system that works very well, and clients continue to be amazed and happy with the results. Culture and leadership style are key.

Nature can also teach us so many lessons about *direction*. Plants grow, and so do your employees. You only get a 'borrow' of them for a limited time, and to expect to hold them in a holding pattern forever is just foolish.

Let them flourish, learn and grow, and if they have outgrown their position and there is no further opportunity for advancement, welcome the fact that you have had a great employee for 8 years or whatever, and move on.

The old saying about training your team. What if I train my team member and she leaves? What if I don't train her and she stays, may be a more appropriate question to ask?

Think of employees like a lake. If the lake has nothing flowing in or out it becomes stagnant. If your company is totally stagnant with employee movement that is also bad. A reasonable incoming of new life and others who are ready to move on is also a good thing. No need to cross your fingers!

— CHAPTER 13 —
Training That is Never Implemented

When will the penny drop? I wonder how many course materials have sat in a cupboard and have never been opened again? Plenty, plenty, plenty.

Why? Was it because the course or training was no good?

Perhaps sometimes. However, I believe that there are at least another couple of reasons why.

Maybe the training course was brilliant (and expensive), but the person who attended can't or won't try and implement it. The reasons are many but often include work politics, resistance to change or 'rock the boat'. Sometimes it is just plain uncomfortable to change things.

The person attending the course was attending it for the wrong reasons. To climb the company ladder, you need the following qualifications, and provided you have attended this course then it will assist you in filling in with a big tick in the selection criteria box for that sought-after promotion.

There is a massive disconnect between attending training courses and implementing them.

Teachers are not coaches.

Trainers have a different mindset to implementers.

Does that make them bad? No, of course not! The problem lies in the misconception of management that sending someone on a training course will fix the rotten culture and dreadful communication in your organisation.

Great course. Why is the implementation going to be zero? It may be because the person who persuaded the boss to let them go on the course was the wrong one in the first place. He/she wanted the kudos, a day/week out of the office, and being able to put that big tick in the selection criteria box, for the juicy promotion.

Potential net results of the training course can be summarised as follows:

– Company out of pocket
– Wrong person set up in line for promotion
– Team further disillusioned, disengaged
– Discretionary effort further eroded
– All rather depressing! What can we do about it?

The company must start out with the basics, and that is through a proper analysis of the team. What I absolutely love doing is helping business owners/managers/directors to understand *in depth* who are the right people to promote and educate.

This team must be identified, nurtured and assisted to implement what they have learnt on these courses, or else it will all have not only been a waste of time and money, but potentially further eroded the culture.

Why did Peter Drucker say that 'Culture eats strategy for breakfast?' Because culture is everything and unless you have implementers who passionately live and breathe the culture of your organisation you are missing out big time. You will promote the wrong people. While you are at it, take your selection criteria nonsense and chuck it out the window.

Hire for attitude.

If you go with the selection criteria nonsense, your systems will only allow you to promote the analytical, non-people orientated micromanager types. People are not cogs. They are not a one size fits all solution, and selection criteria is only a tool, and an ineffectual one at that. Selection criteria is a cop out, a back-up excuse mechanism that can be blamed when the new hire doesn't work out.

Before you send that next employee on that training course, consider the outcome you want to see delivered from their attendance.

– CHAPTER 14 –
Compassion

What dawns on you when you hear that word compassion?

Google it and the synonyms that come up are pity, sympathy, feeling, fellow feeling, empathy, understanding, care, concern, solicitude, solicitousness, sensitivity, tender-heartedness, soft-heartedness, warm-heartedness, warmth, love, brotherly love, tenderness, gentleness, mercy, mercifulness, leniency, lenience, tolerance, consideration, kindness, humanity, humaneness, kind-heartedness, charity, benevolence.

Whatever the definition, there is a massive need for it right now around the globe. When you read about literally millions of people leaving what was their homes and walking hundreds and hundreds of kilometres with only hope in their hearts for a better life, does it not fill your heart with compassion? Then there are the people living in border towns who are overrun with the influx of these sad and desperate people, who also need compassion.

Bring it back home to where you are. Can you or I be more compassionate to our fellow human beings? Sometimes I assume that my clients are okay, my friends are okay and my family is okay, but are they? I am working on being more compassionate with each and every one of them. Spread the compassion is what is burning in my heart.

There is so much 'noise' and 'gum bumping' about stuff that is either irrelevant or ill-conceived. For example, 'Thought Leadership' seems to be the current fad. Last year the buzz-word was 'Integrity'. Before that 'Synergy' and so it goes on.

How about making 'Compassion' the real word for a real world that is crying out for it.

Compassion is an unlimited resource.

Let's spread it today!

– CHAPTER 15 –

The Power of Intention

That is me in the picture above, by the way, happy as can be, with the car of my dreams, and even the cheeky number plate as well! Goodness, how did that happen?

You know Usain Bolt didn't wake up one day and say, 'I am entering the Olympics and going to not only win, but break crazy world records.' It was no accident, it was his *intention*.

Plenty has been written about goals and goal setting. Unfortunately, in the process, many people have become discouraged when their goals didn't work out.

Why would that be?

I liken it to a recipe. Who wrote the recipe? Did that recipe consistently work right? Of course, if you are missing one key ingredient, or you add too much of the wrong ingredient, or take too long in the cooking process, it won't work. It's just like in life when we dream up negative excuses, procrastinate and devalue our own abilities. Things end up not working out, leaving you feeling discouraged and despondent.

What *not* to do.

Stop pushing! Push, push, push does *not* work! Trust me on that one, as I spent years trying that one! Learn to *allow,* with incredible gratitude.

In order to get the things you want there are some essentials. But firstly, you need to look at the four main *reasons* why your goals *don't* work out:

Are they simply the wrong goals? Is there unclear focus?

No clear action plan? Mental hang-ups and barriers?

Identify which of these apply to you and *remedy* the situation.

Next, you must *write out* your goals. I remember listening to the highly successful baker Tom O'Toole speaking, and he stated very emphatically that if you don't have written goals then your goals don't exist. He attributes his successful bakery in country Victoria in part to having written goals.

But that is still not enough!

Here are some other *key ingredients*:

The goals must be written *correctly.*

Passion. This is so important. If your goal does not fire you up with supreme passion, it is probably the wrong goal. You don't get into *motion* without *emotion* (a John Flettism!)

Visualise. Reflect. When you achieve a goal, cherish having achieved that goal with *gratitude*. Be kind both to others and yourself. Do you berate yourself? Stop it! If you catch yourself saying things to yourself that you would never say to your best friend, then stop it!

Remember that your will-power is so much less effective than your *imagination*. Why did Albert Einstein say that *imagination* is greater than knowledge? Start floating your desires instead of sinking them. Think about that one for a bit. Spend 80% of your time thinking and 20% doing, for better results (John Flett).

Of course, most of us start off bogged down in the 'how to' before we have set our *intention*. Anytime a goal has not come about this could be the one basic omission. Now that your goals are starting to line up, check in to make sure your *intention* is clear. It is so important how you set the intention as well…all things that I work with in depth with my clients.

When the intention is clear, the mechanism will appear.

For some extra reading, Dr Wayne Dyer has an excellent book on THE SEVEN FACES OF INTENTION which gives you some additional great clues about intention.

Correct knowledge is the key to unlocking goal achievement. Make no mistake about it, goal setting works. It works amazingly well, but you must do it correctly, *with intention*.

My final words: Go for it! I would love to help you because it fills me with joy to see you successful and supremely happy.

– CHAPTER 16 –
A Bully in a Sneaky Disguise?

Bully, Bully, Bully

Workplace bullying in Australia is at epidemic proportions. It is costing the country billions of dollars and inflicting dreadful psychological damage on the victims and their families.

When will it *stop*? How can we *identify* them?

There are certain key indicators which should set alarm bells ringing to management at all levels (indeed, if they are not guilty themselves of workplace bullying!)

Here are a few key indicators that bullying may be going on, and if cumulatively these are happening in your workplace, you can bet your boots you have bullying in full swing.

High turnover of staff

A lot of excuses coming from the mouth of the same suspected bully

Suspicious denials from the same person

A high number of 'blame game' coming from the same person

The suspected bully has a 'mixed-up' personality profile. (That is why you employ me to profile your prospective employee *before* you employ trouble)

Morale is low for no apparent reason

Sick leave is high

You feel a tension in the air and low energy when you walk into that department; you can almost smell the fear.

There is a general uneasiness in the team without any solid reference to back up why

The suspected bully is a micromanager, keeping key information away from the team for no good reason. A control freak. Fear and minimal communication are two of his/her favourite tools. Mixed messages are the norm.

The bully uses prolonged 'silences' and uses that to build tension

The bully behaves differently when person key staff members are around – often is quite charming to them

The problem also lies in the fact that often the bullied person just simply leaves, and not wanting to cause trouble or have anything more to do with the organisation, does not report the bullying or complain in any way. Worse still, and also a frequent occurrence, complaints may have been made to management, but they were either ignored or treated as unimportant.

The bullying then continues unabated. In fact, there is a feeling of smug contempt by the perpetrator at the failure of the bullied ex-employee to have managed to combat him/her successfully.

This is so common, that it often passes as acceptable behaviour, which it most certainly is not. In fact, it is so common that I know of many workplace bullying situations personally. They repeatedly occur in a wide variety of different industries, unchecked. Chatting to my hairdresser, it turns out that she had been the subject of dreadful bullying while a young apprentice. It seems that everywhere I turn, bullying is rife!

Then, of course there is the medical fall-out from bullying. I sometimes wonder what the fish in Moreton Bay are eating with the residue of Prozac, Zoloft and Lovan just to name a few of the medications floating around out there, often prescribed by doctors to ease the suffering of the bullied person. Where else can they turn for help?

One doctor allegedly said that half of his patients were on Prozac and the other half should be. If true, then this is truly an awful situation.

What do you think? Who do you know who has suffered from bullying at work? Why is it happening?

Perhaps it is ignorance. As an example, are employees aware that an eye roll and a flick back of the hair could be bullying?

Silence is also often used as a powerful bullying tool.

Have we unwittingly nurtured bullies from the babies born in the '60's and '70's when it became trendy to never say no to your child? Could it be that the horrid little monster who was the one getting his/her own way by screaming in a tantrum to get lollies at the supermarket checkout, has now become the highly experienced, adult bully?

– CHAPTER 17 –
Great Employee vs One That Should Be Employed Elsewhere

Perhaps you have a big 'fat seagull' in your employ, just pecking away, being paid by you?

Can you spot him/her?

Think about your place of work and where you sit in regards to *employee engagement*. This list of characteristics may help you to recognise the difference between great employees and those who should work elsewhere.

Great Employee

- *Loves* his/her work
- *Loves* helping colleagues as well as co-operating with suppliers and customers
- Energetic
- Totally motivated
- Think creatively as well as working creative ideas into a logical result
- Not in it just for the money
- On top of his/her work – never too busy to not be able to take time out
- Loyal leader
- Thinks company and other employees first
- Inspirational
- Encourages and leads but never *manages* other people
- Growth mindset
- Open to new ideas
- Values and accepts critique and constantly looks at new ways to improve
- Coachable
- Humble
- Honest
- Reliable
- Strategic
- In-depth thinker
- Win/win negotiator
- Great understanding of allowing for differing personalities
- Prosperity attitude

Employee who should work elsewhere

- Negative thinker
- Closed to new ideas
- Resists change
- Sees things only his/her way
- Selfish
- Proud
- Only here for the money attitude
- Manipulative
- Devious, trouble-maker
- Poor communicator
- Glass half empty
- Energy drainer
- Disengaged
- Stressed
- Too busy to help anybody else
- Maintains secrecy and holds onto power
- Resists systemisation
- Political
- Spends the bulk of his/her time sucking up to the boss
- Hides key information
- Hates his/her work
- Self-first, company last
- Looks at protecting himself/herself first
- Not interested in growth
- Has an 'I know' attitude
- Closed mindset

- Criticises and attempts to *manage* people
- Uncoachable
- Disengaged
- Moody and unhelpful

I know which employees I would prefer to employ!!!

— CHAPTER 18 —

Books for the 21st Century

The Good Reads and Fun Classics

Good Reads

THE SLIGHT EDGE by Jeff Olson

An important good read; practical advice, and a must for anyone who wants to improve long term.

FRIEND AND FOE by Adam Galinsky and Maurice Schweitzer.

Written by two Professors this book only came out in Sept 2015, and is well researched as well as well written. A stand out top book.

RETURN ON CHARACTER by Fred Kiel.

The man behind Intel's success.

MAVERICK by Ricardo Semler

Has been out for a while, it is THE book that is changing how we interact so much better with employer/employee relationships. A must read.

THE 50 BEST ARTICLES OF STEVE PAVLINA

This guy has worked on himself so much it shows up in his researched information. Trails around in the middle for a bit, but some useful information there.

THE GIFTS OF IMPERFECTION by Brene Brown

Loved her earlier books and she does not disappoint here either.

HEALTHY BRAIN, HAPPY LIFE by Wendy Suzuki and Billie Fitzpatrick

A different book from a lady who has led one interesting life.

WHAT EVERY BODY IS SAYING by Joe Navarro and Martin Karlins

Written by an ex FBI interrogator, Joe gives you a different take on Body Language. Whilst many of us have been exposed to Allan Pease's books, his take is quite different, especially the bit about 'feet don't lie'. A good read.

DARING GREATLY by Brene Brown

This lady's sheer honesty takes your breath away. Good book.

THE ASTONISHING POWER OF EMOTIONS by Esther & Jerry Hicks

It may be a bit 'out there' for some of you, but I enjoyed it.

OUT OF OUR MINDS by Sir Ken Robinson

I couldn't put this book down. Absolute cracker and a must read. If you don't buy any others on this list buy this one.

DESTINY OF SOULS by Michael Newton

Incredible book but if you are a devout Christian/Atheist/Muslim/Buddist Religion devotee give it a swerve as it may upset you. Personally, I really enjoyed it.

BRANSON: BEHIND THE MASK by Tom Bower

Along with many others I thought Branson was a great guy, until I read this book. Oh my! If only half of what is in this book is true, then Branson is a real shocker. I don't think Tom Bower was or will be on Branson's Christmas list this or any year!

MINDSET: HOW YOU CAN FULFIL YOUR POTENTIAL by Professor Carol Dweck

I am a big fan of her work and this easy read well researched book is a must read.

THE HONEYMOON EFFECT by Bruce Lipton

THE BIOLOGY OF BELIEF by Bruce Lipton

Both these books by Bruce Lipton are excellent. When I read the first one, I just had to buy and read another!

LEADERS EAT LAST by Simon Sinek

Very 'pop' currently, some of his science is questionable in my opinion from other work I have read especially in regards to the brain. Nevertheless, a good book. The problem often lies in that authors of books have not necessarily started up and run successful businesses before putting pen to paper – and it shows in their writing.

BLOCKCHAIN REVOLUTION by Dan and Alex Tapscott

You need to know about Bitcoin and now Blockchain. A major disrupter of the 21st Century.

THE ONE THING by Gary Keller and Jay Papasan

Loved the principle behind this book and in a complicated world, breaking stuff down to one thing is great.

DELIVERING HAPPINESS by Tony Hsieh

The man behind online retailer Zappo's success. Love this guy's 'out there' work.

BUSINESS MODEL GENERATION by Alexander Osterwalder & Yves Pigneur

This book was recommended to me by one of my outstanding clients. It's a handbook for visionaries, game changers, and challengers striving to defy outmoded business models and design tomorrow's enterprises.

Fun and Classics

NINETEEN EIGHTY-FOUR by George Orwell

ANIMAL FARM by George Orwell

You must read both these books in your lifetime!

THE PICTURE OF DORIAN GRAY by Oscar Wilde

Brilliantly written and eloquently expressed – gee Dorian was a right b..! A must read.

OLD MAN AND THE SEA by Ernest Hemingway

You can almost picture Hemingway sitting in his favourite bar in Cuba penning this novel. Classic all-time great book – an easy read too.

EAST OF EDEN by John Steinbeck

This is a classic novel and it's easy to understand why. You get gripped by the pure evil of the female main character!

LOST HORIZON by James Hilton

The mythical Shangri-La – it's a cool book. I wonder if James Redfield the author of The Celestine Prophecies was inspired by this novel.

– CHAPTER 19 –

Looking for Work/Life Solution

Looking for a Work/Life Balance?

Doh! By the very expression one must be out of whack with the other! I must admit that because I enjoy my work so much, I had a client say to me 'when are you going to take your work John, as you seem to be enjoying yourself too much. Are you on holiday all the time?"

Work/life *integration* is what we should be 'shooting for' as my Texas friend would say! If you are doing what you love to do, you will never work another day in your life! It's all about finding out where your strengths lie and what you enjoy doing, and going for it. As for working towards retirement, why would you do that? That is ultra-dumb in my book, as when you reach that goal then what happens? Yes, you got it – you die!

Why not do something different instead? Enrol in the Hug Academy perhaps? Have a hug with your nearest and dearest and release some good oxytocin into your system. If you have been trying to manage your team, and on the seesaw of playing at trying to achieve a work/life balance, there is a much better way.

Here are some clues to how to achieve work/life integration. *Developing systems* is a no brainer, and a start. That can end up being a bit of an obsession but the big one in my book, the elephant in the room, is *the people aspect* and what they are doing at work.

Firstly, why are you – the owner or CEO, doing work tasks that should be delegated?

This is like a lady I knew who was very good at selling and able to make consistently $200 an hour. She was complaining that she hated spending 15 hours a week doing book-keeping, which she was not very good at. Simple solution – employ a book-keeper at $50 an hour and make a net $150 hour extra. Bonus, because the bookkeeper was very good at her work she did the job better and faster taking only 8 hours to do the work! The further bonus is she was much happier because she was only doing the work she enjoyed!

That is just the start.

Ask yourself, what do you think you are worth? Are you only worth cleaner's wages? If you are cleaning your office, that is what you have valued your time as being worth. Are you really that good at cleaning anyway?

I had a client who told me that he found cleaning was very therapeutic for him as it gave him thinking time. He felt that no cleaner would do as good a job as he does. This revelation resulted in him maintaining a very clean Unit. From this he developed some great business ideas utilising his passion.

The skill is doing more with less, and finding out how to develop your leadership skills, which we can help you with as well. There is always a better way of doing things, and a way to deliver you more time and money. This is the fun aspect of my work as I have a mantra to 'find my fee fast.' I've yet to find a business that hasn't left plenty of money 'lying on the table!'

We are creatures of habit. Sometimes we just stop thinking, and go into this robotic state of same old, same old, without looking for alternative ways of doing things. Is that you?

Belief systems are also important as they come into play every time. Are you fully aware of your own belief systems and how they colour your daily life?

Our parents, teachers, mentors and influencers taught us some excellent stuff such as making sure we looked both ways when crossing the road, but they also ingrained some rather peculiar ideas. These can be near impossible to change! These are the ones that hold us back and give us the ideas of chasing silly things such as work/life balance notions.

'Remember your station in life' was one that was drummed into me as a kid! Uh?

— CHAPTER 20 —
Negotiation

Negotiation is something we all do all day, every day but how many people really know how to negotiate successfully?

Not many I would venture to say.

When I say successfully, most of us have heard the expression win/win negotiation, which in simple terms means that both parties walk away happy and contented with the outcome.

But how many times have we come away from a negotiation feeling sick in the guts, cheated or feel we could have done better. That is a win/lose negotiation. We feel lousy and cheated. And sometimes it is made worse by the apparent gloating of the victor!

Of course, there is more to negotiation than just the outcome. The most important question I want to address is this:

What if I could learn more about negotiation than the other side, don't you think it would place me at an advantage?

Of course, it would.

Without this knowledge, negotiation would be like stumbling along in the dark, tripping over the flagstones and potholes at some unearthly hour of the morning, as I did when taking the picture at the top of this post in Angkor Wat! When the sun comes up (metaphorically speaking), through being educated in negotiation, you start to see things clearly avoiding the pitfalls that come of 'not knowing what you don't know.' This can take you out of the losing end of a negotiation!!!

Firstly, and most importantly, there are only 3 variables in any negotiation. These are:

Power, Time and Information

Power is what we all want in a negotiation. How do we get it?

They say knowledge is power...yes that does help! It is very important to prepare yourself well prior to the negotiation, ensuring that you have as much power on your side as possible.

Time is an interesting one. Determining if they are under *time* pressures or deadlines is a key to the successful negotiation. If the opposing party has time constraints, you have a definite advantage.

Through intelligently gathering as much *information* about the party you are negotiating with, you put yourself in a powerful position. The other party's information they have garnished prior to the negotiation will also be a factor in how the negotiation ends up.

So, next time you are involved in a negotiation, be sure to run these three pillars of negotiation through your mind. Stacking these three variables in your favour is key to a successful negotiation outcome.

Negotiation in practice is exciting, particularly watching and hopefully, steering, the interplay of the three pillars in action.

Here are a couple of common *examples* of negotiations: If you are stopped for speeding by a traffic policeman, clearly, he has the *power*, normally too he has plenty of *time*, and if the *information* of your speed is on his speed camera screen, you are pretty much doomed, and he knows it. He is most likely to win this negotiation! However, if, as happened to me once many years ago, he is writing you a ticket and his ticket book has no sheets left in it on which to write the ticket, you may well get off. I did!!

What about the traffic policeman suddenly gets radioed to go elsewhere? The *time* element has then swung in your favour. Or if his speed camera suddenly goes on the blink, as with my luck with the empty ticket book, you may just have a slight chance of getting off!

It always amuses me when sellers state categorically, 'We don't negotiate on our prices'. I think to myself 'really?' What happens when *time* comes into play, and the items have sat on the shelves and competitors have developed a better or cheaper product, and that *information* becomes widely available to you, the buyer?

Do you think our 'not negotiable sellers' will suddenly start to change their tune? *Time* and *information* start to play a big part. At the risk of not selling this merchandise at all, they can become very negotiable!

Conversely, think carefully if you are considering taking on a large Government department. They have a lot of innate *power*!!

Now that I have brought this to your attention you will start to see this pattern of *Power, Time and information* everywhere.

These are the first basics of negotiation.

If you would like to find out more, or be assisted with your individual negotiation needs, we run a series of negotiation workshops in Brisbane, Australia. These go into a lot more depth and provide understanding of the underpinning concepts as well as the processes. They are very practical in nature. One of the outcomes of our workshops which gives us the most pleasure is when delegates put into action their learnings and give us feedback of their amazing results.

www.ingramcontent.com/pod-product-compliance
Lightning Source LLC
Chambersburg PA
CBHW070427180526
45158CB00017B/907